INTERNATIONAL OUTBREAKS

SARS

Heather C. Hudak

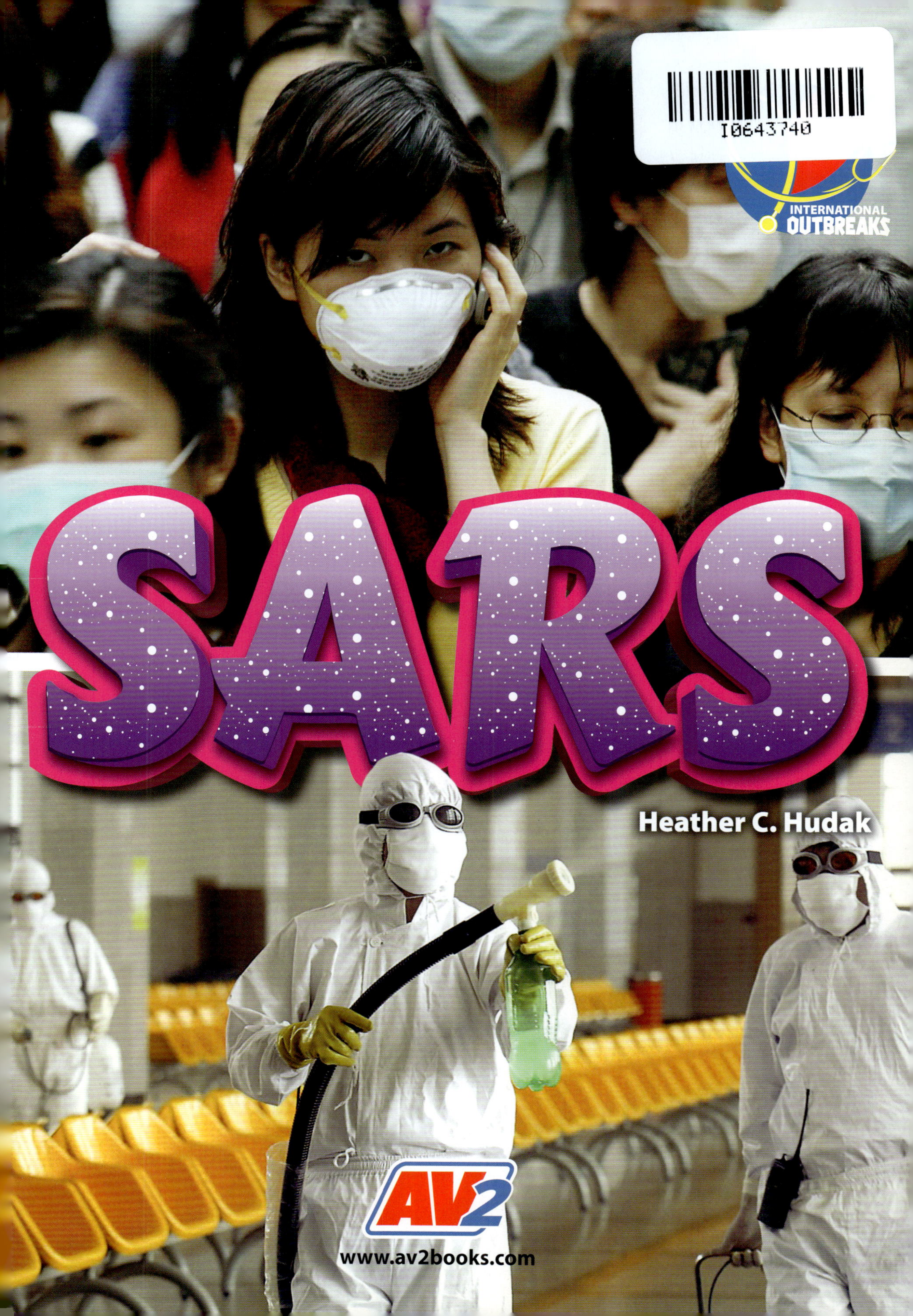

AV2
www.av2books.com

Step 1
Go to **www.av2books.com**

Step 2
Enter this unique code

MLCEAA54F

Step 3
Explore your interactive eBook!

AV2 is optimized for use on any device

Your interactive eBook comes with...

Contents
Browse a live contents page to easily navigate through resources

Audio
Listen to sections of the book read aloud

Videos
Watch informative video clips

Weblinks
Gain additional information for research

Try This!
Complete activities and hands-on experiments

Key Words
Study vocabulary, and complete a matching word activity

Quizzes
Test your knowledge

Slideshows
View images and captions

... and much, much more!

INTERNATIONAL OUTBREAKS

SARS

CONTENTS

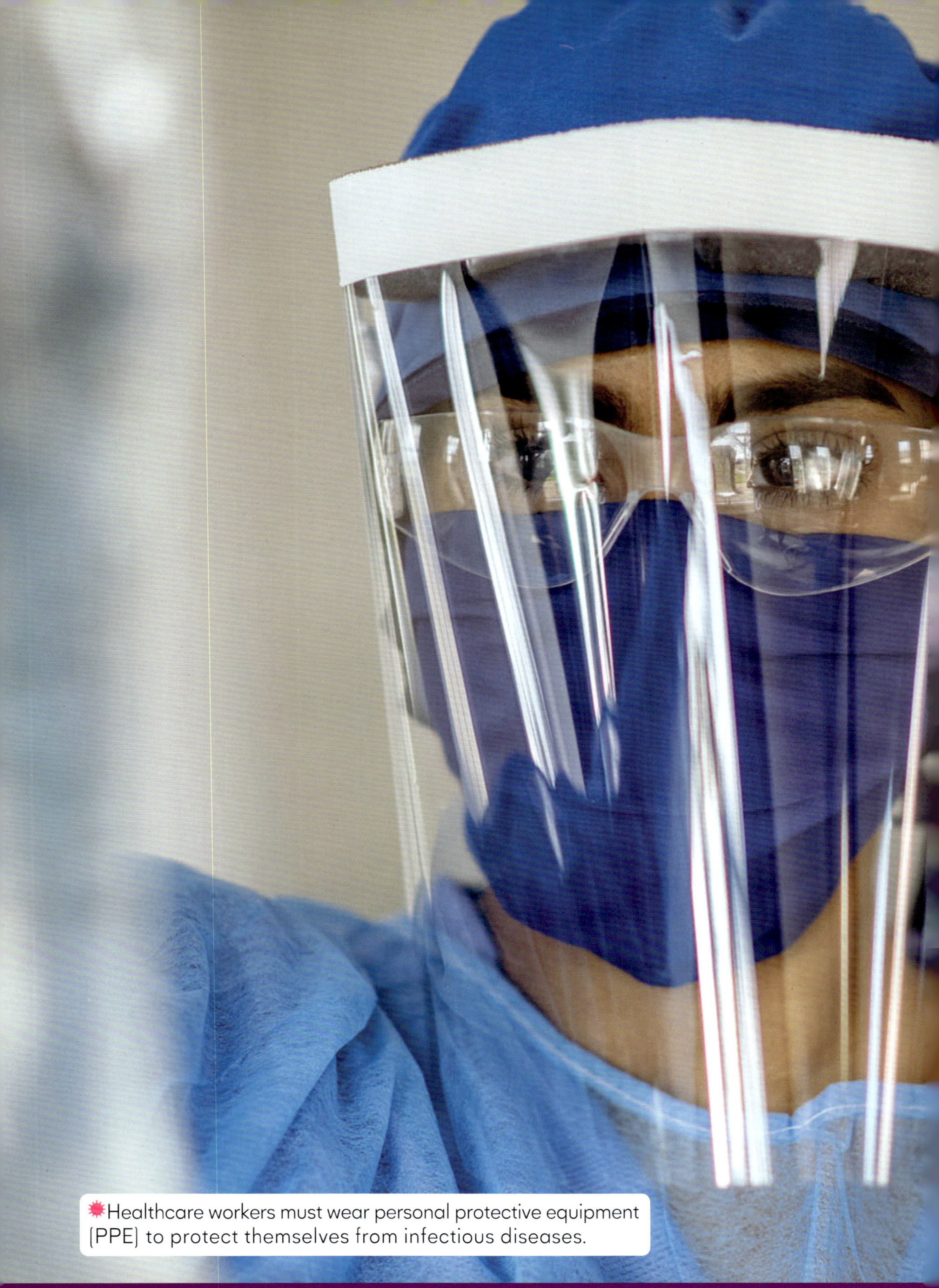

Healthcare workers must wear personal protective equipment (PPE) to protect themselves from infectious diseases.

Breaking Out

Tiny germs called **viruses** are all around us. They live in all kinds of places. Some viruses make people sick. They can even be deadly. It is important for scientists to learn as much as they can about viruses so they can help protect people from **diseases** caused by viruses. One way that scientists do this is by tracking different types of viruses. They count how many cases of each disease happen at a certain time and place. Then, they compare the numbers to past years. They figure out how many cases are normal. This tells them what to expect for future years.

An outbreak happens when there are more cases than usual. Some outbreaks end after a few days. Others last for months or years. Outbreaks may take place in just one small area. They can also spread to many larger areas. An epidemic happens when a virus spreads very quickly to many people. It usually takes place over a larger area than an outbreak. This is what happened in 2002. A new virus called SARS started to **infect** people in China. It then quickly spread to more than two dozen countries in different parts of the world.

FAST FACT

Sometimes, doctors cannot **contain** an epidemic. It spreads to many parts of the world and affects a large part of the world's population. This is called a pandemic.

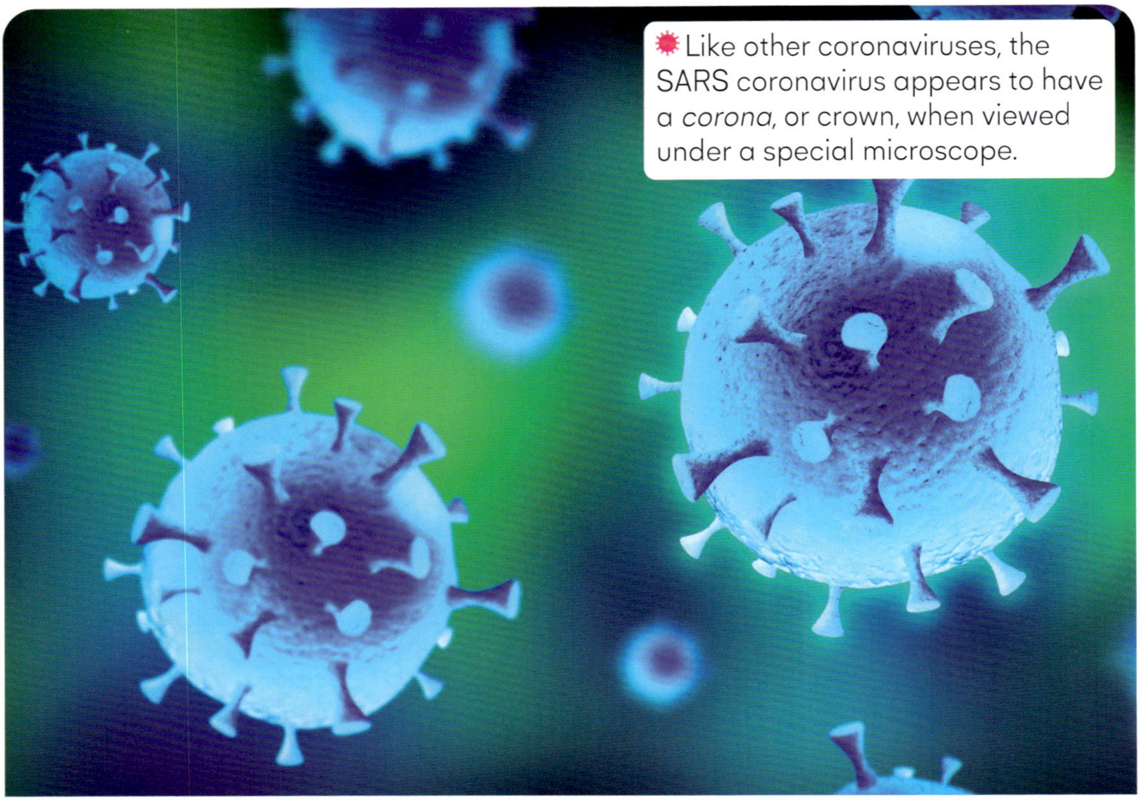

Like other coronaviruses, the SARS coronavirus appears to have a *corona*, or crown, when viewed under a special microscope.

What Is SARS?

SARS stands for severe acute respiratory syndrome. It is an infectious disease. SARS attacks a person's **respiratory system**. Most people have mild symptoms at first. The symptoms become worse over time. Some people with SARS cannot breathe well on their own. The first cases of SARS took place in November 2002. People in the Guangdong province of China began to get sick. At first, doctors thought the people had pneumonia. It took some time for them to discover that it was a new type of disease.

Doctors had never seen anything like SARS before. They found it was caused by a new type of coronavirus. This is the same kind of virus that causes the common cold. However, SARS is much more deadly. Scientists believe the SARS virus jumped from an animal to a human. The virus has been found in **civets** and other animals.

Railway stations and other public spaces were frequently disinfected during the SARS epidemic.

Handwashing with soap and water for 20 seconds can help stop the spread of viruses.

Spreading the Virus

SARS is a **contagious** disease. It spreads from person to person and can infect anyone. An infected person must come in close contact to give another person SARS. The virus is found in droplets that come out of an infected person's nose, mouth, and throat. The droplets get into the air when the person coughs, sneezes, or talks.

Droplets can travel about 3 feet (0.9 meters). They may land inside another person's nose, mouth, or throat. The droplets remain in the air for a short time. Then, they fall to the ground and land on objects such as doorknobs, phones, and keyboards. The virus can spread when people touch a contaminated object and then touch their nose, eyes, or mouth. This is why it is so important for people to wash their hands often.

Using disinfectants to clean objects that are frequently touched can get rid of droplets and germs.

High Risk

People who live with someone who has SARS are at high risk of catching the virus. They are more likely to breathe in the same air as the infected person. Health workers who care for people with SARS also face a high risk of infection. SARS is very unlikely to infect people who walk by an infected person on the street. People are also not likely to get SARS if they sit across the room from an infected person for a short time.

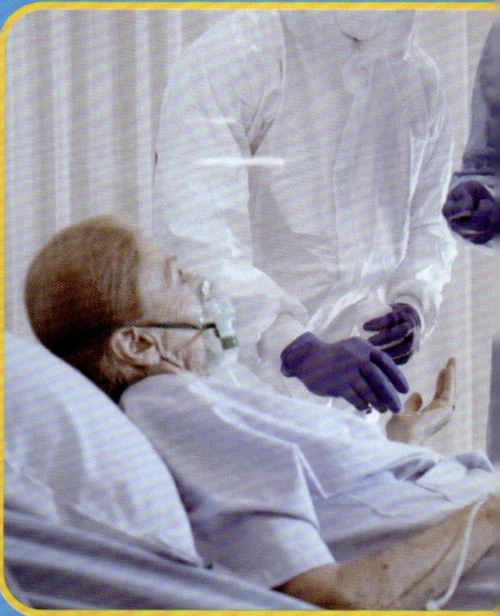

Signs, Symptoms, and Treatment

It can be hard to tell if a person has SARS. The disease has many of the same symptoms as the flu. SARS starts with a fever. Then, people start to show symptoms such as headaches, chills, diarrhea, or sore throats. Some people have body aches or feel tired. After a few days, they get a cough. Breathing problems show up about two to ten days after a person gets SARS. Many people develop pneumonia. About 10 to 20 percent of people with SARS need help to breathe. They may need to use a device called a **ventilator**.

SARS begins to spread once a person shows signs of the disease. People with SARS are most contagious in their second week of feeling sick. About one-third of cases get better on their own. Other SARS patients may need to be hospitalized to get better. More than 10 percent of patients die. There is no cure for SARS.

Doctors watch ventilators to make sure that a patient's oxygen levels do not fall too low.

Preventing the Spread of SARS

Wash your hands often
with soap and water,
or use hand sanitizer

Clean and disinfect
frequently touched
objects and surfaces

Stay at home
if you are sick

Wear a face mask

Avoid close contact
with people who are sick

Cover your mouth and nose
with a tissue or your sleeve
when coughing or sneezing

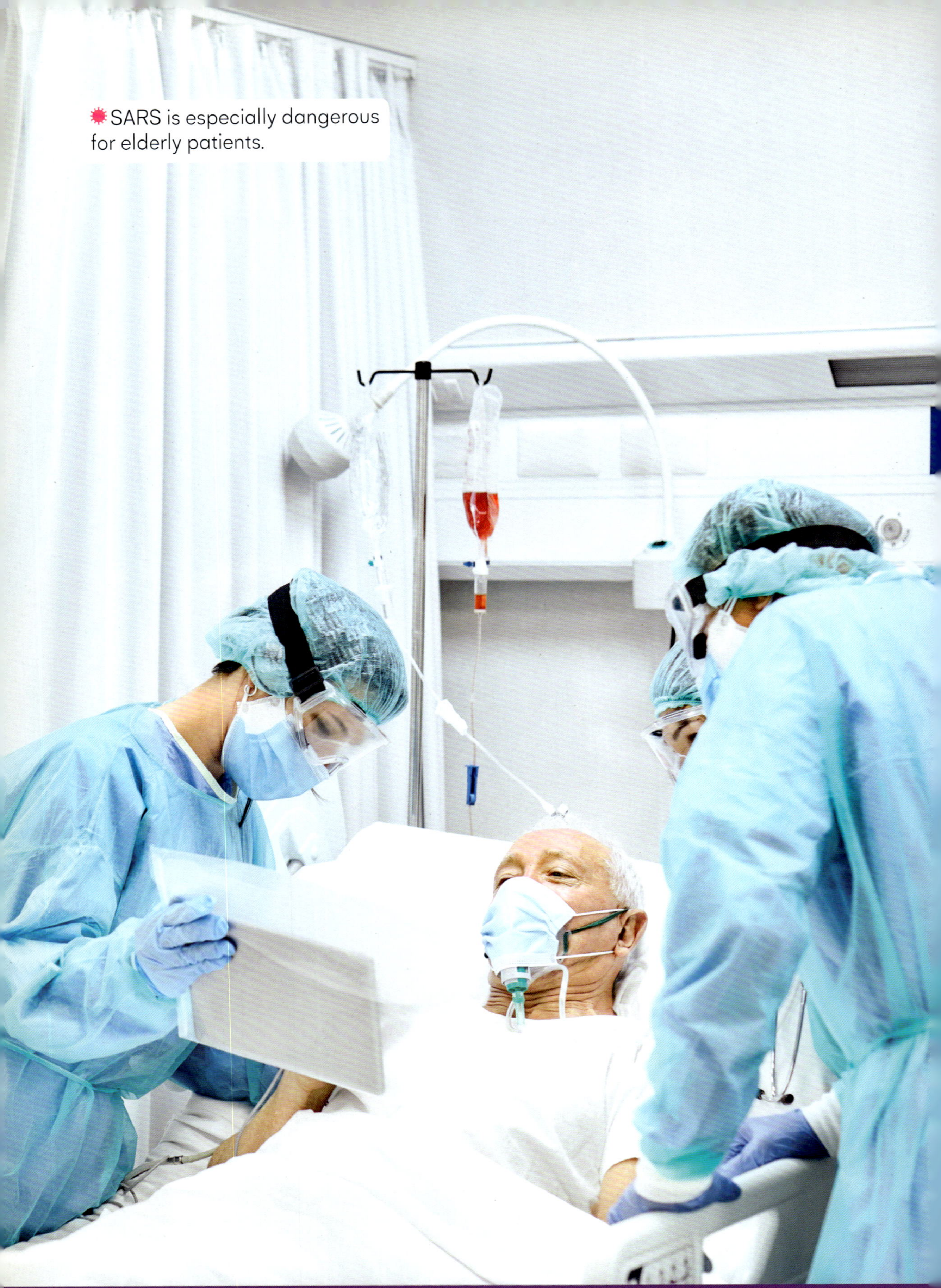

SARS is especially dangerous for elderly patients.

SARS Outbreak, 2002 to 2003

In late 2002, a 45-year-old man became the first known victim of SARS. The man's wife, niece, aunt, and uncle all became sick, too. The family lived in Foshan City in Guangdong province. Soon, the virus spread to other parts of the province. By January 2003, the illness reached Guangzhou, the capital of Guangdong province. The disease infected many people there.

No one outside of China knew about SARS for months after the first case. In February 2003, the **World Health Organization** (WHO) was informed about it. There were 305 cases in Guangdong province at the time. Then, more cases started to show up in other parts of the world. WHO began to **investigate**.

Super Spreader

A doctor in Guangzhou treated many people who had SARS. Toward the end of February, he went to Hong Kong for a wedding and checked into a hotel. He did not feel well, but he still went shopping and sightseeing. The next day, he went to the hospital. He died a few weeks later. While in Hong Kong, he infected many people with SARS. Almost 80 percent of the Hong Kong cases can be traced back to him.

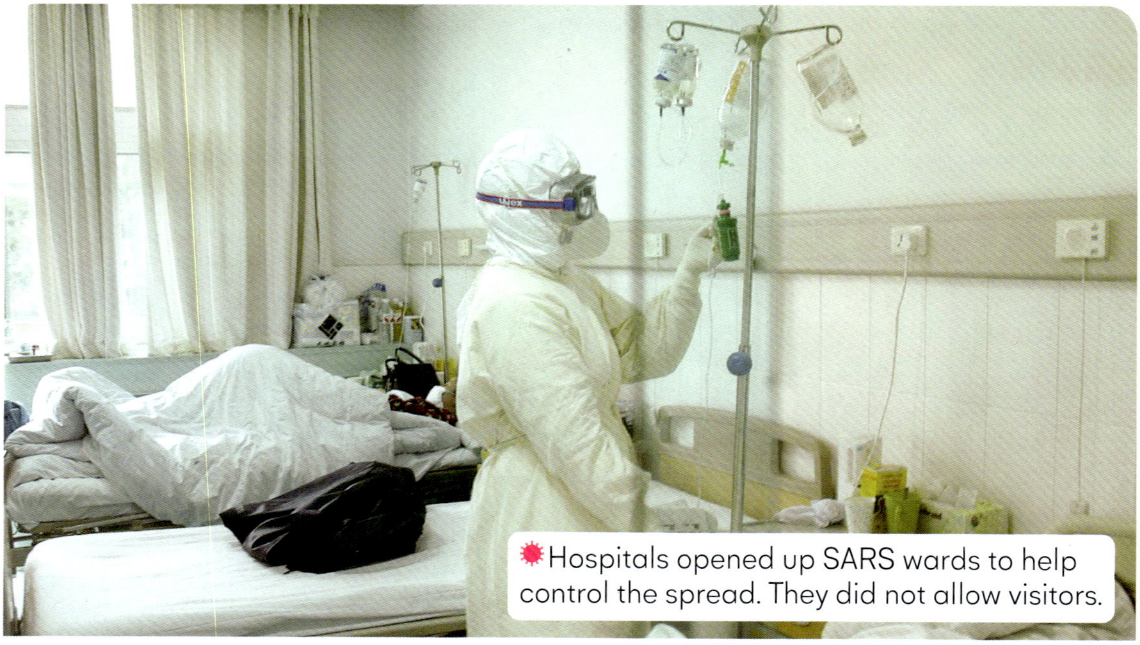

Hospitals opened up SARS wards to help control the spread. They did not allow visitors.

Global View

Many people stayed at the same hotel as the doctor from Guangzhou. One of them was a 78-year-old woman from Toronto, Canada. She got on a plane and flew home. The woman did not know she was sick at the time. She died a few weeks later. Many members of her family fell sick, too. The disease then spread quickly to others. Other travelers who stayed at the same Hong Kong hotel became sick as well.

WHO sent out a global outbreak alert on March 12, 2003. The virus had spread to Canada, Germany, Taiwan, Thailand, the United Kingdom, Hong Kong, Vietnam, and Singapore. Countries around the world began to prepare for outbreaks. They put people who were sick in **quarantine**. This helped stop close contact with others. Some countries put travel restrictions in place. Others closed schools. Hospitals began strict practices for treating the sick.

Mapping the SARS Outbreak from November 2002 to July 2003

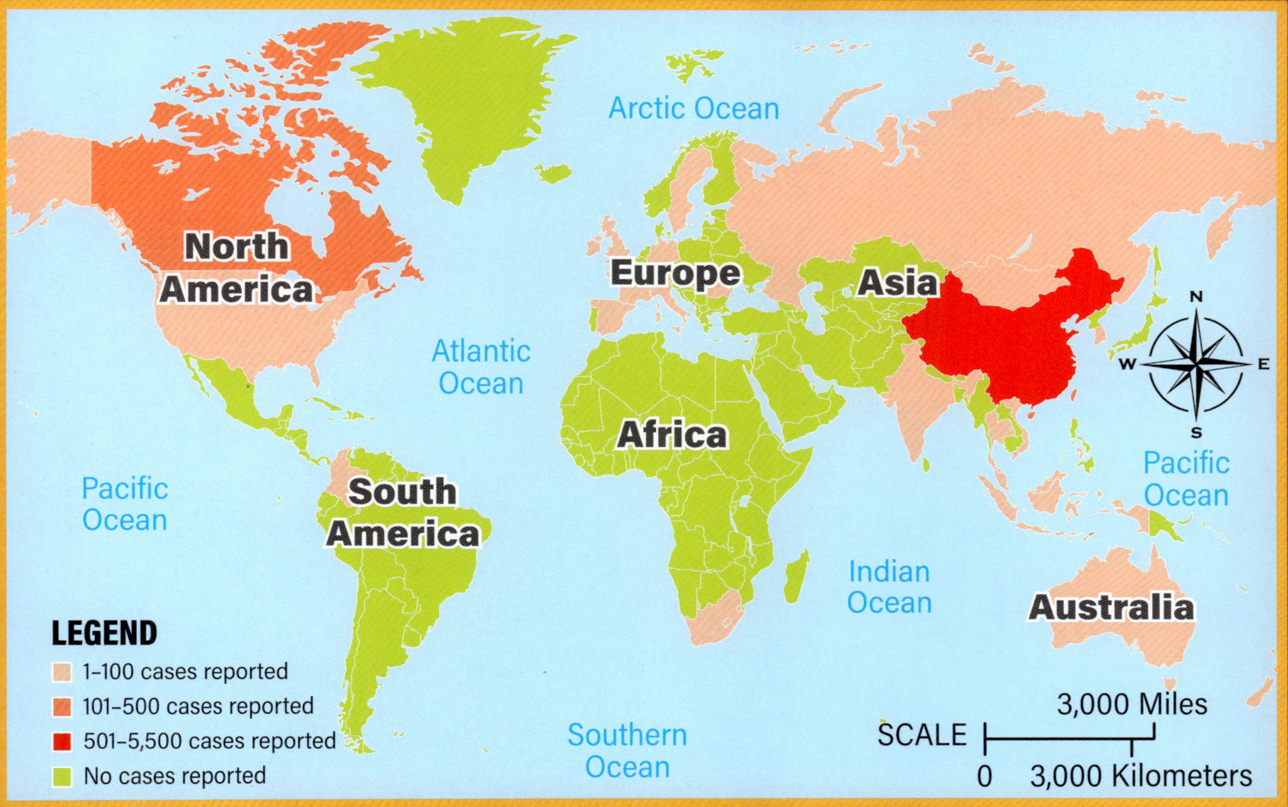

People with certain diseases must be **quarantined** until they recover. In **April 2003**, SARS was added to a list of these diseases.

By **June 2003**, the spread of the SARS virus **slowed down**. Life began to go back to normal.

On **July 5, 2003**, WHO said that the global SARS **outbreak was contained**.

Science and Research

Doctors need to do tests to tell if a person has SARS. Sometimes, they swab the person's nose or throat. Other times, they take blood. The samples are sent to a lab. Scientists check the samples for signs of the virus. Chest x-rays are used to look for signs of pneumonia.

During the epidemic, the best way to stop SARS was to prevent its spread. People who had SARS stayed home and did not go to work or school. They avoided contact with others for at least 10 days after their symptoms went away.

FAST FACT

In late 2019, a new type of coronavirus was discovered. It caused the COVID-19 disease. COVID-19 quickly spread around the world. The disease has a lower **mortality rate** than SARS, but it spreads faster and more easily. By April 2020, millions of people were infected. Hundreds of thousands of people had died.

Preventative measures, such as handwashing and wearing masks, helped stop the spread of SARS.

People around the world celebrated the end of SARS with parades and concerts.

SARS Today

By late July 2003, there were no new cases of SARS. The epidemic was over. More than 8,000 people around the world had been infected with SARS. Of them, 774 died.

Today, the risk of SARS is very low. Since 2003, there have not been any major SARS outbreaks. However, there have been a few cases of the virus in China. Lab workers have also come in contact with samples of the virus. SARS taught countries a great deal about how to prepare for virus outbreaks.

SARS Cases from November 2002 to July 2003

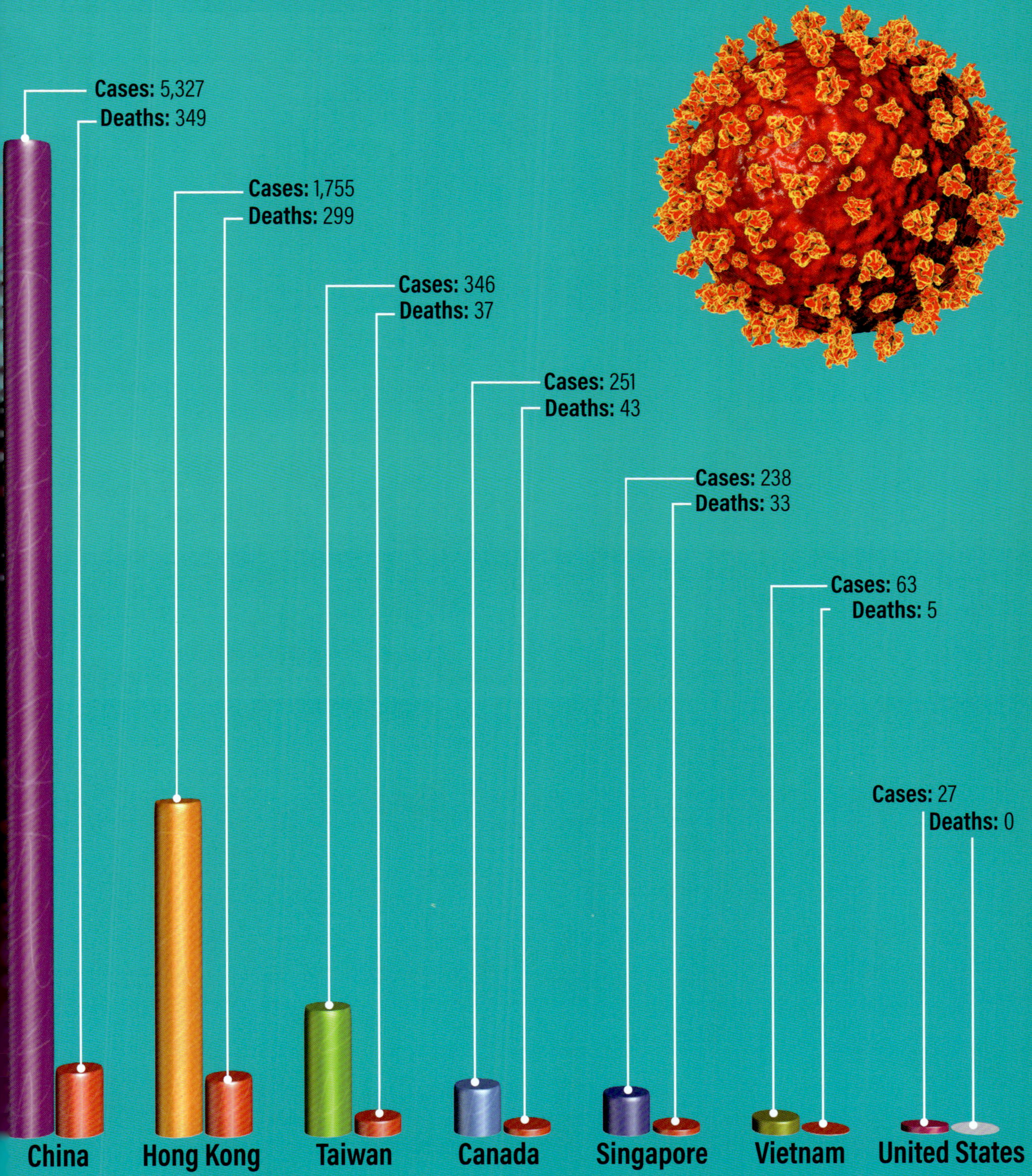

SARS Timeline

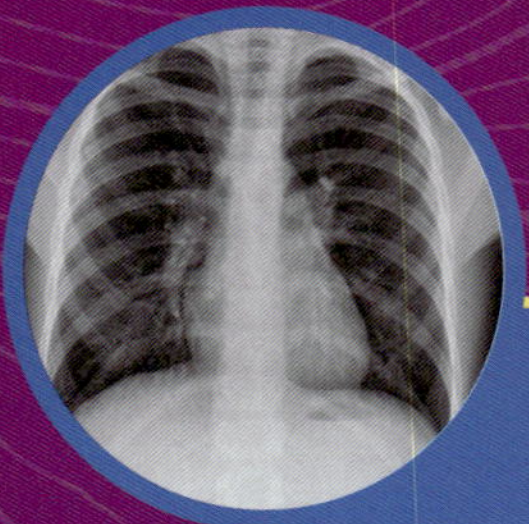

November 16, 2002

A new disease appears in China. Doctors think it is a type of pneumonia.

February 21, 2003

A doctor who has been infected by the disease travels to Hong Kong. He infects many others at his hotel.

March 16, 2003

WHO officially names the disease Severe Acute Respiratory Syndrome, or SARS.

March 18, 2003

Doctors report SARS cases in Canada, Germany, Taiwan, Thailand, the United Kingdom, Hong Kong, Vietnam, and Singapore.

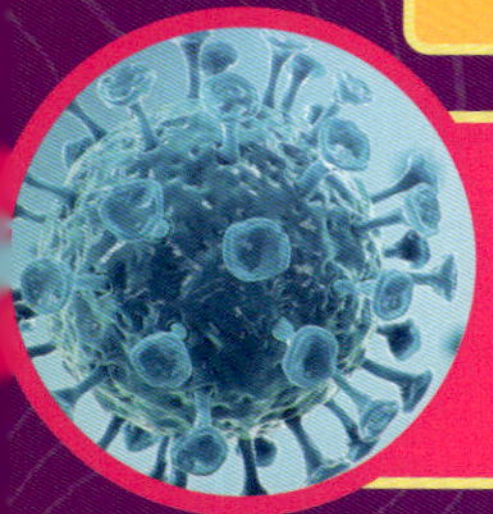

April 16, 2003

WHO discovers that SARS is caused by a new type of coronavirus.

July 5, 2003

WHO says the SARS outbreaks are contained. Countries should still watch carefully for any new cases.

2020

There are no known cases of SARS in the world.

ACTIVITY
Infecting Others

Some viruses are very common. Millions of people are infected by the flu virus each year, for instance. Others, such as the SARS virus, are rare. Still, both the flu and SARS spread easily. Try this activity to see how viruses spread quickly from one person to many others.

What You Need

- Plate
- Flour
- Toy blocks

What to Do

1. Cover the plate in flour. Press one hand into the flour.
2. Play with the blocks for three to five minutes.
3. Hold out your hands. Is there flour on both hands?
4. Look at the blocks. Can you see flour on them? Some may have just a little flour on them. That still counts.
5. Take a look around the area. Are there other objects with flour on them? Do you have flour on your clothes?
6. Did you notice how quickly the flour spread from just one of your hands to so many other objects? This is how some viruses spread from one person to other people and objects.
7. What do you think would have happened if you washed your hand after you pressed it into the flour? Would that have stopped the flour from spreading?

SARS QUIZ

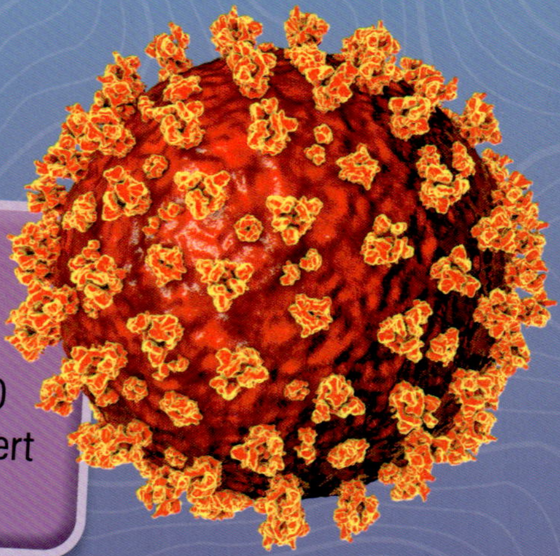

1
Where did the SARS outbreak begin?

2
When did WHO issue a global alert about SARS?

3
How many people around the world had SARS?

4
How does SARS spread?

5
Is there a cure for SARS?

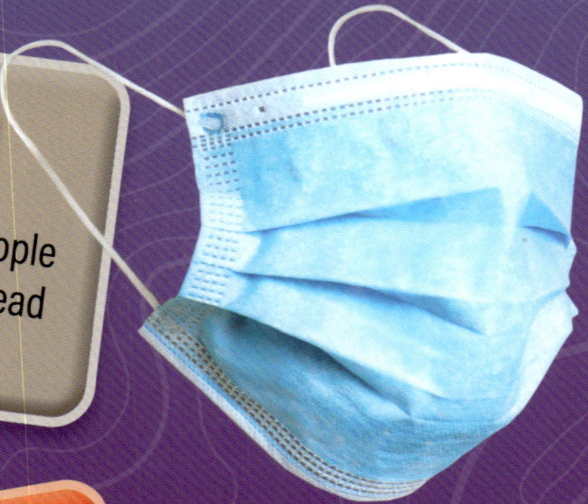

6
How can people stop the spread of SARS?

7
How did SARS get to other parts of the world?

8
How do doctors test for SARS?

ANSWERS

1. Guangdong province in China
2. March 12, 2003
3. More than 8,000
4. Through contact with droplets from an infected person or contaminated objects
5. No
6. By staying home when they are sick, washing their hands often, and avoiding touching their eyes, nose, and mouth
7. Travelers who stayed at a hotel in Hong Kong carried the SARS virus with them to other parts of the world
8. Nose or throat swabs, blood tests, and chest x-rays

Key Words

civets: small, catlike, meat-eating mammals found in Africa and Asia

contagious: moves easily from one person to another

contain: keep under control

diseases: illnesses that have certain signs and symptoms

infect: contaminate a person or object with a disease-causing germ

investigate: to look into something to try to find the facts

mortality rate: the percentage of deaths among people with a certain disease

quarantine: strict isolation to prevent the spread of a disease

respiratory system: a group of organs and tissues inside the body that let people breathe, such as the nose, throat, and lungs

ventilator: a device that helps people breathe by moving air in and out of their lungs

viruses: very small germs that get inside the body and spread

World Health Organization: an organization that sets health standards and guidelines that many countries follow

Index

Get the best of both worlds.

AV2 bridges the gap between print and digital.

The expandable resources toolbar enables quick access to content including **videos**, **audio**, **activities**, **weblinks**, **slideshows**, **quizzes**, and **key words**.

Animated videos make static images come alive.

Resource icons on each page help readers to further **explore key concepts**.

Published by AV2
14 Penn Plaza, 9th Floor
New York, NY 10122
Website: www.av2books.com

Library of Congress Control Number: 2020943892

ISBN 978-1-7911-3242-2 (hardcover)
ISBN 978-1-7911-3243-9 (softcover)
ISBN 978-1-7911-3244-6 (multi-user eBook)
ISBN 978-1-7911-3245-3 (single-user eBook)

Printed in Guangzhou, China
1 2 3 4 5 6 7 8 9 0 24 23 22 21 20

082020
101119

Art Director: Terry Paulhus Project Coordinator: Priyanka Das

Every reasonable effort has been made to trace ownership and to obtain permission to reprint copyright material. The publisher would be pleased to have any errors or omissions brought to its attention so that they may be corrected in subsequent printings.

The publisher acknowledges Getty Images, iStock, and Shutterstock as its primary image suppliers for this title.